EMMI THE PINK ELEPHANT

-Book Three-

Written and Illustrated by

Barbara Klein

Printed in the United States of America

ISBN-13: 978-1729626405

10 9 8 7 6 5 4 3 2

Empire Publishing

www.empirebookpublishing.com

All Scripture passages are the author's own paraphrase.

CHAPTERS

EMMI, THE PINK ELEPHANT AND BILLY, THE BUNNY

A large truck carrying animals for the pet store drove over a big bump.

Out jumped a little bunny. He looked around for a second and then hopped quickly off into the jungle.

Monty, the Monkey, and his friends were playing in the trees when they saw the Bunny.

"Hello. What's your name?" They asked.

"Billy," said the Bunny in a soft voice.

"Come and play with us," cried the Monkeys.

Billy, the Bunny, made a tiny hop toward the Monkeys, but then stopped.

"What's the matter?" Asked Monty, the Monkey.

Billy, the Bunny, couldn't answer. He just hopped back into the jungle.

The next day, Chester, the Cheetah saw Billy, the Bunny, hiding in the bushes.

"Hello," said Chester, the Cheetah, "You're new around here aren't you? Where do you come from?"

I... I... I don't know," said Billy, the Bunny, softly.

"Would you like to meet my friends?" Asked Chester, the Cheetah.

"Yes, I guess so," replied Billy, the Bunny.

But after Billy, the Bunny took a few hops, he stopped and then turned and quickly hid again.

Paddy, the Parrot, had been flying and watching Billy, the Bunny. Paddy, the Parrot landed near him and asked, "Why are you so shy? What's the matter?"

Billy, the Bunny, couldn't answer. He wanted to talk and he so much wanted to make friends, but he didn't know how.

Monty, the Monkey, Chester, the Cheetah, and Paddy, the Parrot decided they must tell Emmi, the Pink Elephant about Billy, the Bunny.

When Emmi, the Elephant, heard, she went right away to find Billy, the Bunny.

She found him sitting under a big tree all alone and sad.

"Hello, said Emmi, the Pink Elephant, "I would like to be your friend."

Billy, the Bunny, looked up at Emmi, the Pink Elephant.

"I am not like everyone here and I don't know how to be a friend, "Billy, the Bunny said.

"Come with me. My friends and I will teach you how to be a friend, "said Emmi, the Pink Elephant.

Billy, the Bunny, could see the love in the eyes of Emmi, the Pink Elephant, and so he slowly hopped along side of her.

Emmi, the Pink Elephant, talked with Billy, the Bunny, and made him feel loved. For the first time in his life, he began to be okay. He began to believe that he had a friend. He began to feel accepted just as he was.

Then Emmi, the Pink Elephant, took out her book that she always carries with her.

"May I read you something?" She asked Billy, the Bunny, and she read:

"Do not be afraid... Believe me... I want to make you my friend."

"Would you like to meet Jesus? Asked Emmi, the Pink Elephant, He will help you to not be shy anymore if you will give him your heart."

So, Billy, the Bunny, knelt with Emmi, the Pink Elephant, and asked Jesus to come into his heart

"Now come and meet your new friends," said Emmi, the Pink Elephant.

Billy, the Bunny, hopped along beside Emmi, the Pink Elephant. At first, he wanted to hop away when he saw Emmi's friends, but this time he knew that Jesus loved him and Emmi, the Pink Elephant, loved him too. Now he was okay.

It didn't matter what he was or where he came from. He knew he didn't need to be afraid. He knew that if he would just be himself, he would make friends.

And so he did.

Billy, the Bunny, hopped all over the jungle making friends. Many of the animals had never seen a bunny before and they thought he was very special.

And, of course, he was.

NOTES TO ADULTS

The Scripture references in this story are found in: John 14:1 and John 15:15.

QUESTIONS YOU MIGHT TALK ABOUT WITH THE CHILDREN

1. Why was Billy, the Bunny so shy?

2. What helped him to become a friend?

3. Do you have a friend who is different than you? Does it matter?

4. How do you act toward someone who is different?

5. How would Jesus act toward them?

EMMI, THE PINK ELEPHANT
AND
THE JUNGLE OLYMPICS

Emmi, the Pink Elephant, Chester, the Cheetah, Monty, the Monkey, and Paddy, the Parrot were on their way to the Jungle Olympics.

They were all excited about seeing the Monkeys play basketball,

and the Zebras run at the track,

and the **Hippos** race at the pool.

But, as they were coming to the stadium, they heard a lot of commotion and saw all the animals running around.

"What's going on?" Asked Chester, the Cheetah.

"George, the Gorilla and his gang have showed up," cried a very frightened Antelope, "They have chased the Monkeys from the basketball court, and ran the Zebras off the track, and drove the Hippos out of the pool. They have taken over the Jungle Olympics.

Where is this George, the Gorilla?" Asked Emmi, the Pink Elephant, "I'm going to see him!"

"But he and his gang will jump all over you!" Cried the Antelope.

"George, the Gorilla, is nothing but a bully," said Emmi, the Pink Elephant, "and the only way to deal with a bully is to stand up to him."

So, Emmi, the Pink Elephant went off to find George, the Gorilla and his gang.

When George, the Gorilla and his gang saw Emmi, the Pink Elephant coming, they yelled.

"Here comes that Pink Elephant. Let's go after her. We can take her out!"

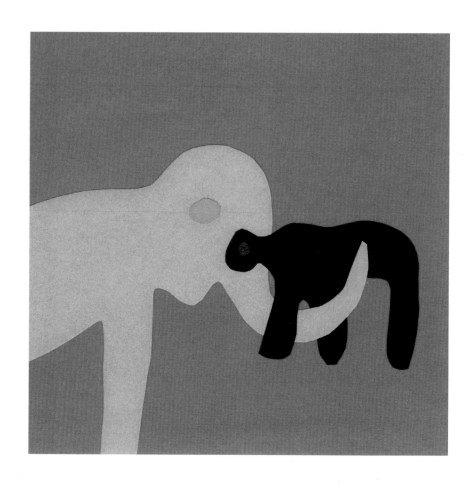

But, when they ran to Emmi, the Pink Elephant, she took George, the Gorilla in her trunk and began to lift him high in the air and swing him around.

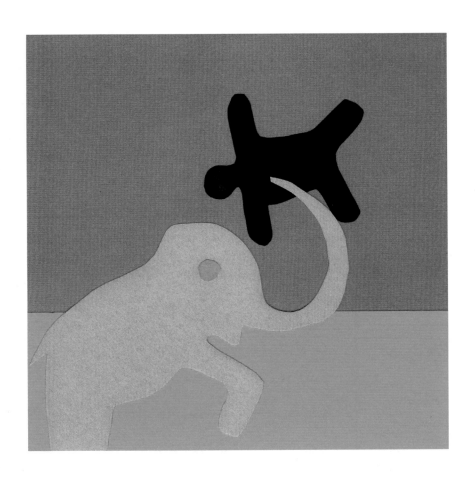

"Let me down! Let me down!" Cried George, the Gorilla, "I'm sorry. Please let me down."

So, Emmi, the Pink Elephant set him down on the ground.

"Are you really sorry?" Emmi, the Pink Elephant asked George, the Gorilla.

"Oh, yes I am," said George, the Gorilla, "I'll never do it again!"

Emmi, the Pink Elephant, wrapped her trunk around George, the Gorilla, with a big elephant hug and said, "You are really a good Gorilla, George. The animals will like you. You don't have to be a bully."

Then Emmi, the Pink Elephant got out
the book that she always carries with her
and read:

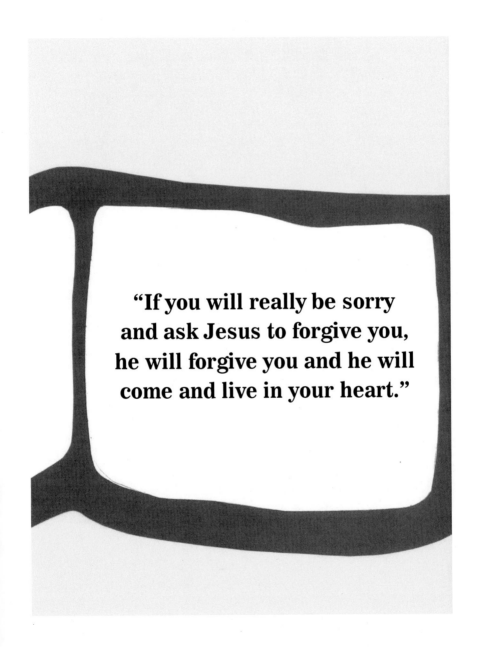

"If you will really be sorry and ask Jesus to forgive you, he will forgive you and he will come and live in your heart."

"Would you like to ask Jesus to come into your heart?" Emmi, the Pink Elephant asked George, the Gorilla.

"Yes, I would," said George, the Gorilla.

So he and all the Gorillas in his gang knelt down and asked Jesus to forgive them and to come into their hearts.

From then on, everything went fine at the Jungle Olympics. George, the Gorilla and his pals (for they were not a gang anymore) played on the volleyball team.

Emmi, the Pink Elephant, Chester, the Cheetah, Monty, the Monkey, and Paddy, the Parrot had great fun watching the Monkeys play basketball, the Zebras run at the track, and the Hippos race in the pool. It was an exciting day for everyone.

And, they all cheered when George, the Gorilla and his volleyball team won a gold medal.

NOTES TO ADULTS

The Scripture references in this story are found in: 1 John 1:9 .

QUESTIONS YOU MIGHT TALK ABOUT WITH THE CHILDREN

1. Where were Emmi, the Pink Elephant and her friends going?

2.What was the problem at the Jungle Olympics?

3.What did Emmi, the Pink Elephant do about George, the Gorilla?

4. Do you know anyone like George, the Gorilla?

5.How would you like to help him or her?

32704634R00024

Made in the USA
Columbia, SC
12 November 2018